THE WORLD'S WORST NATURAL DISASTERS

THE WORLD'S WORST
TORNADOES

by John R. Baker

CAPSTONE PRESS
a capstone imprint

Blazers Books are published by Capstone Press,
1710 Roe Crest Drive, North Mankato, Minnesota 56003
www.mycapstone.com

Library of Congress Cataloging-in-Publication Data
Names: Baker, John R. (John Ronald), 1989–
Title: The world's worst tornadoes / by John R. Baker.
Description: North Mankato, Minnesota: Capstone Press, 2017. | Series: Blazers.
   World's worst natural disasters | Audience: Grades 4 to 6. | Includes bibliographical
   references and index. | Description based on print version record and CIP data
   provided by publisher; resource not viewed.
Identifiers: LCCN 2016000445 (print) | LCCN 2015049414 (ebook) | ISBN
   9781515717966 (eBook PDF) | ISBN 9781515717881 (library binding) |
   ISBN 9781515717928 (paperback)
Subjects: LCSH: Tornadoes—History—Juvenile literature.
Classification: LCC QC955.2 (print) | LCC QC955.2 .B34 2017 (ebook) |
   DDC 551.55/309—dc23
LC record available at http://lccn.loc.gov/2016000445

Summary: Describes history's biggest and most
   destructive tornadoes from around the world.

Editorial Credits
Aaron Sautter, editor; Steve Mead, designer; Jo Miller,
media researcher; Tori Abraham, production specialist

Photo Credits
AP Images, 18–19, Pavel Rahman, 12–13; Getty Images: AFP
Photo/Ross Tuckerman, 22–23, Hulton Archive/Topical Press
Agency, 6–7, Jerry Laizure, 8–9, Jordan Mansfield, 16–17,
Zachary Roberts, 20–21; Newscom: EPA/Ken Blackbird, 24–25,
UPI/Tom Uhlenbrock, 14–15, ZUMA Press/Ken Stewart,
10–11, ZUMA Press/St Petersburg Times, 28–29; Shutterstock:
EmiliaUngur, 4–5, leonello calvetti, cover, 3, 31, Martin Hass,
cover, Minerva Studio, 26–27

Design Elements
Shutterstock: solarseven, xpixel

Printed in China.
007700

TABLE OF CONTENTS

NATURE'S POWER UNLEASHED

THE EF SCALE

5
4
3
2
1
0

The Enhanced Fujita (EF) Scale measures a tornado's strength. An EF0 tornado is the weakest. It does the least amount of damage. An EF5 tornado is the most powerful. It causes the most destruction.

Trees snapped in half. Roofs ripped off buildings. Cars tossed around like toys. What did this? A tornado! These powerful twisting storms cause damage around the world every year. Hang on tight. It's time to learn about the world's worst tornadoes.

RANKING

0	1	2	3	4	5
65 to 85 mph (105 to 137 kph)	86 to 110 mph (138 to 177 kph)	111 to 135 mph (178 to 217 kph)	136 to 165 mph (218 to 266 kph)	166 to 200 mph (267 to 322 kph)	more than 200 mph (322 kph)

Wind Speeds (miles/kilometers per hour)

TRI-STATE TERROR

Location:
Missouri, Illinois, Indiana

Date:
March 18, 1925

EF Rating:

5
4
3
2
1
0

On March 18, 1925, one tornado set a record. The monster twister stayed on the ground for an incredible 219 miles (352 km)! It destroyed entire towns across three states. The Tri-State Tornado was the deadliest in U.S. history. It killed 695 people.

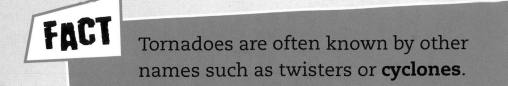

cyclone—a fast spinning column of air

MONSTER IN OKLAHOMA

Location:
Oklahoma City, Oklahoma

Date:
May 3, 1999

EF Rating:

5
4
3
2
1
0

May 3, 1999, was a dark day in Oklahoma City. A giant, 1-mile- (1.6-km-) wide tornado destroyed entire neighborhoods. Streets were filled with broken trees and shattered homes. The giant twister caused more than $1 billion of damage. It killed 36 people.

The Oklahoma City tornado had wind speeds up to 318 miles (512 km) per hour. It was the fastest tornado wind speed ever recorded.

1974 SUPER OUTBREAK

Location:
Midwest and eastern United States

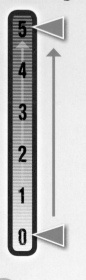

Date:
April 3–4, 1974

EF Rating:

5
4
3
2
1
0

Huge storms swept across North America on April 3 and 4, 1974. They created a record **outbreak** of more than 140 tornadoes. The twisters caused death and destruction in 13 U.S. states and Canada. At least 65 of those twisters were rated EF3 or higher.

FACT

The 1974 Super Outbreak killed more than 300 people. The twisters also caused more than $600 million in damage.

DISASTER IN BANGLADESH

Location:
Dhaka,
Bangladesh

Date:
April 26, 1989

EF Rating:

5   unknown
4
3
2
1
0

The world's deadliest tornado occurred on April 26, 1989. The killer twister hit near Dhaka, Bangladesh. About 1,300 people died as it tore through thousands of homes. Another 12,000 suffered injuries in the storm.

FACT

The deadly storm in Bangladesh left 80,000 people without homes.

A DIRECT HIT

Location:
Joplin, Missouri

Date:
May 22, 2011

EF Rating:

5
4
3
2
1
0

A nightmare visited Joplin, Missouri, on May 22, 2011. A giant EF5 twister plowed a path of destruction through the middle of the town. It killed more than 150 people. It also did $2.8 billion in damage. It was the costliest tornado in history.

FACT

In April 2011, more than 750 tornadoes were recorded in the United States, setting a new record.

BRITISH OUTBREAK

Location:
Great Britain

Date:
November 23, 1981

EF Rating:

5
4
3
2
1
0

No place in the world is safe from tornadoes. On November 23, 1981, a record 105 twisters hit Great Britain. The county of Norfolk saw at least 13 tornadoes touch down. Most of them were weak and didn't last long.

Tornadoes in the United Kingdom are rated using the International Tornado Intensity Scale. The weakest storms have a T0 rating. The strongest are rated T11.

TOPEKA TWISTER

Location:
Topeka, Kansas

Date:
June 8, 1966

EF Rating:

5
4
3
2
1
0

It was a **humid** summer day on June 8, 1966. That evening a giant EF5 tornado headed straight for Topeka, Kansas. It tore a 22-mile- (35-km-) long path through the city. The fierce storm damaged 3,000 homes. It killed 16 people. Another 500 were injured.

The tornado in Topeka caused $250 million in damage. Today that price would be more than $1.6 billion. It was one of the costliest twisters in U.S. history.

—damp and moist

CANADIAN CYCLONE

Location:
Regina,
Saskatchewan,
Canada

Date:
June 30, 1912

EF Rating:

5
4
3
2
1
0

In 1912 Regina was a thriving city in Saskatchewan, Canada. On June 30 a tornado destroyed much of the city. The cyclone flattened homes. It reduced brick buildings to rubble. The twister left 2,500 people with no place to live.

FACT The Regina twister killed 28 people. That's more than any other tornado in Canada's history.

ONE POWERFUL STORM

Location:
Bucca, Australia

Date:
November 29, 1992

EF Rating:

5
4
3
2
1
0

Most tornadoes in Australia aren't very strong. But a powerful EF4 twister struck the small town of Bucca on November 29, 1992. It had wind speeds of 166 miles (267 km) per hour. The storm also carried baseball-sized **hail**. It was the strongest tornado ever seen in Australia.

FACT

On November 4, 1973, a tornado ripped up more than 1,300 buildings near Brisbane. It caused more damage than any other twister in Australia's history.

hail—balls of ice that fall during a thunderstorm

A SUPERSIZED MONSTER

Location:
Hallam,
Nebraska

Date:
May 22, 2004

EF Rating:

5
4
3
2
1
0

The widest twister ever recorded hit Hallam, Nebraska, in 2004. This supersized EF5 monster stretched 2.5 miles (4 km) wide. Mud and **debris** from the small town's buildings filled the streets.

FACT

The Hallam tornado destroyed 150 homes. It also wiped out the town's schools, post office, churches, and office buildings.

A TORNADO FACTORY

Location:
southeastern
United States

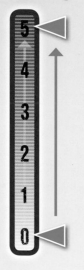

Date:
September 15–18,
2004

EF Rating:

5
4
3
2
1
0

Hurricanes often form dozens of tornadoes. In 2004 Hurricane Ivan set a record for the most twisters created by a hurricane. When Ivan hit the southeastern United States, it formed 117 tornadoes over four days.

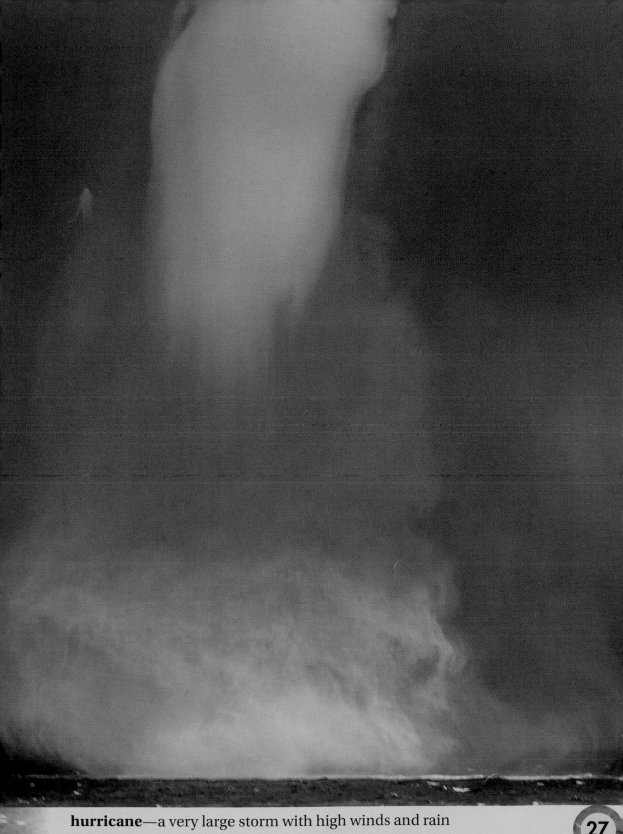

hurricane—a very large storm with high winds and rain that forms over an ocean

TORNADO SAFETY

When a **tornado warning** sounds, head for the nearest basement or storm shelter. Get under a stairwell or stay in a hallway. Most of all, keep away from windows. Tornadoes are nature's fiercest storms. Knowing where to go will help keep you safe from their awesome power.

DISASTER EMERGENCY KIT

An emergency kit can be very helpful in case of a tornado. A good kit should include these items:

- ✔ first-aid kit
- ✔ flashlight
- ✔ battery-powered radio
- ✔ extra batteries
- ✔ blankets
- ✔ bottled water
- ✔ canned and dried food
- ✔ can opener
- ✔ whistle to alert rescue workers

tornado warning—an alert issued when a tornado has been seen or is expected soon

GLOSSARY

cyclone (SY-klohn)—a fast spinning column of air

debris (duh-BREE)—the scattered pieces of something that has been broken or destroyed

hail (HAYL)—balls of ice that fall during a thunderstorm

humid (HYOO-mid)—damp and moist

hurricane (HUR-uh-kane)—a very large storm with high winds and rain that forms over an ocean

outbreak (OUT-brake)—a large number of events that occur in a certain area

tornado warning (tor-NAY-doh WOR-ning)—an alert issued when a tornado has been seen or is expected soon

READ MORE

Challoner, Jack. *Eyewitness Hurricane & Tornado.* DK Eyewitness. New York: DK Publishing, 2014.

Garbe, Suzanne. *Threatening Skies: History's Most Dangerous Weather.* Dangerous History. North Mankato, Minn.: Capstone Press, 2014.

Rustad, Martha E. H. *Tornadoes: Be Aware and Prepare.* Weather Aware. North Mankato, Minn.: Capstone Press, 2015.

INTERNET SITES

Facthound offers a safe, fun way to find Internet sites related to this book. All of the sites on Facthound have been researched by our staff.

Here's all you do:
Visit *www.facthound.com*
Type in this code: 9781515717881

 Check out projects, games and lots more at **www.capstonekids.com**

CRITICAL THINKING USING THE COMMON CORE

1. Tornadoes often kill people and cause huge amounts of damage. Which tornado was the deadliest in history? Which one was the costliest? (Key Ideas and Details)

2. Explain what you should do if you hear a siren signaling a tornado warning. (Craft and Structure)

3. Look at the chart on pages 4–5. What are the wind speeds for each category of tornado on the EF scale? (Integration of Knowledge and Ideas)

INDEX